Wo[rkbook]

for
It's OK That You're Not OK

A Book by
Megan Devine

Created
By

Cosmic Publications

COSMIC
PUBLICATIONS

Note to Readers

This is an unofficial workbook summary & analysis of Megan Devine's book *"It's OK That You're Not OK"* designed to enrich your reading experience. Buy the original book on Amazon.

Cosmic Publications have not added or removed any information that would change or indicate a different view other than the views and opinions expressed by the author of the original work.

OUR FREE GIFT TO YOU

We understand that you didn't have to buy our summary, but because you did, we are very happy to give you something absolutely free.

Scan the QR Code to get free Access.

Scan me

Table of Contents

How to Use This Workbook

Cosmic Publications has done its absolute best to bring you a comprehensive workbook with summarized chapters of the original for your convenience. Here, you will find Key Takeaways, reflection questions, and action steps for each chapter, plus a Self-Evaluation writing section for your own personal thoughts.

KEY TAKEAWAYS:

The key takeaways are designed to get an overall view of what you should expect to accomplish after each chapter. We recommend reading over the key takeaways as many times as needed to stay focused on the main point of the chapter so that you can better accomplish your goal.

REFLECTION QUESTIONS:

Unlike other workbooks, our questions are about you and not about the information in the book itself. Each question is written to help you evaluate where you are concerning the lessons in the chapter. This workbook is not a "test your knowledge" book. It is a guide to help those that need changes in their life. We recommend you take the time to answer each one honestly, then after some time has passed, come back and answer them again to see where you are. Making photocopies of the questions may be helpful.

ACTION STEP:

It's not enough to just read and write about the lessons learned in the book, but to act so that you can begin to improve your life permanently. In the action step, we recommend attempting the activity within 24 hours of reading the chapter. Even if you have not gone through all the reflection questions, taking steps toward your goal is more important than waiting and perhaps never doing it at all. So, take action right away.

SELF-EVALUATION:

Accountability is essential when trying to make yourself better. In the self-evaluation section, write your experience with each chapter lesson. How did it go? Did you have difficulties? Did you accomplish what you set out to do? Write your thoughts and feelings about what you were able to do with the lesson of the chapter. We hope that this section will be full of positive statements and helpful criticisms if need be.

FINALLY:

It is our opinion that each chapter, along with its corresponding workbook material, be done on a per-week basis. If you can focus on one chapter per week and implement the action step every day, you are more likely to maintain it beyond the workbook. You can change this to a few days if you prefer, but whatever you decide, stick to it. You got this!

It's Ok That You're Not Ok In A Nutshell

Megan Devine's book, It's Ok That You're Not Ok, highlights the grief and pain that came to existence because of the death of a loved one. The purpose of the book is not to heal people who are grieving or fix them. It's not going to put people back on track and move on as if the death that brought about grief did not exist, or never happened. This book will help readers continue living with loss inside them. This book will help readers carry out their daily tasks with the thought of the death still inside them. This book acknowledges that pain over losing that person will always be there, but it provides readers with a chance to understand that their pain will not hinder life's process, or how it goes. This book will help the reader face their demons, and some parts of the book will be much harder than others to go through. These parts, the painful ones, will serve as the best teachers, listeners, and mentors to go through that pain, and they will help the readers understand how to process their grief and how they can live through it.

We're very sorry that you need this book, but we're very happy you've chosen to seek its help.

Part 1
This Is All Just as Crazy
as You Think It Is

Chapter 1:
The Reality of Loss

In the book's first chapter, the author explains that grief and love are two sides of the same coin. There is no loving without grieving. It is the price to pay for a love truly felt. Grief comes about in different forms. It can be the loss of a parent, spouse, child, friend, or family member. It can also be over people you don't really know yet still feel for. The author uses examples from all walks of life to explain that: a mother and wife who lost her life to cancer after an excruciating battle, an athlete who dove into a body of water and came out paralyzed, a volunteer who got hit by a bus or lost his life to a tsunami when he was on a mission in South America, and many more. Grief has no one form; it manifests itself in different situations and can strike when least expected. Grief is brought about after a person experiences a tragic loss of some sort. This loss, the loss a person faces, brings about extreme pain, is something real and alive, and grievers shouldn't just sweep it under the rug.

So what is pain?

Pain is ugly, and there are some kinds of pain that a person cannot really move on from. In fact, in order to deal with pain, the worst thing a griever could do is focus on moving on from it. There's no moving on from pain, simply because what caused that pain (loss) is something that probably changed a person's entire life, maybe even swept the rug from under their feet and was so sudden they just couldn't quite catch their breath afterwards. The loss that occurred put a hold on everything going on in their life. They struggle to carry out even the simplest of tasks, where daily routines become a chore, their limbs feel too heavy, their entire body feels numb, and their thoughts don't have any intelligible pattern.

What is normal?

The author explains that all that is experienced after loss, is normal. This is what grief looks like, and she stresses that it is important to feel all that. A griever would see all their loved ones trying to support them, trying to cheer them up, helping them not dwell on what has happened, and say comforting words to alleviate their pain. But it just gets worse. It is as if they are on a plane, and others are on another one altogether. Here, platitudes and cheerleading do nothing to make grievers feel better. They're extremely useless and only serve to make the griever feel even more helpless and misunderstood. How could others come close to understanding the griever when they haven't faced that kind of loss themselves?

You're not helping

Devine further explains that these condolences are not going to help grievers feel better. In fact, the way culture deals with grief is seriously broken. People believe that avoiding talks about grief is the way to deal with it, just sweeping it under the rug and believing that yes, what has happened is extremely unfortunate, but it's there and it's done, and now it's time to move on. There is nothing wrong with grief; it's a natural response to loss, and grief only exists because love was felt; grief is not some disease that breaks out in a person's body, but it could be just enough to break a person's soul.

Key Takeaway:

The grief, the pain, and all those tumultuous feelings you experienced and are experiencing, they're normal. They will become integrated with your very soul, becoming part of the fabric of your existence.

Reflection Questions:

1. How did your immediate circle react when you experienced loss?

_____

_____

_____

_____

_____

_____

_____

2. How did you feel when your circle reacted that way?

_____

_____

_____

_____

_____

_____

_____

3. What did you wish was different about their reaction?

_____

_____

_____

_____

_____

_____

_____

4. How did you feel when you first experienced the death of a loved one?

_____

_____

_____

_____

_____

_____

5. How did that death affect your life?

_____

_____

_____

_____

_____

_____

_____

Action Step:

Think about your answers to the reflection questions. Do you think your reaction to the loss you've experienced would've been different had your circle given a different kind of reaction, or support? In what ways? For this week, practice telling yourself that it's ok you're grieving, and justify to yourself why. Practice being ok that you are hurting and experiencing pain and don't feel bad about it.

Self-Evaluation:

Journal Entry -- Write key points you felt were helpful in this chapter. Did reading this chapter change your outlook on pain, or the loss you've experienced, in anyway?

_____

_____

_____

_____

_____

_____

_____

_____

_____

_____

_____

_____

_____

_____

_____

_____

_____

Chapter 2:
The Second Half of the Sentence:
Why Words of Comfort Feel So Bad

When a person sees other people sad or upset, they want to be there to fix their problem so that they feel better, and that person would feel better because they helped them. Yet this is not the case here. The one thing the author stresses continuously throughout her book is the fact that grief is not really a problem that should be fixed. There is no solution for grief because grief is not a problem in the first place. Loss is not a problem either. Neither loss nor grief are things human beings experience as problems, which is why the conventional solutions to these never work.

How to fix pain

There is no fixing pain. How could it be fixed when it's a feeling to be felt and not a problem to be solved? The worst part is when people try to make grievers feel better by offering heartfelt condolences. She uses an example of a friend whose father has died to show that when people offer sincere apologies and express sadness over a certain loss, a griever might find their comments mean at best and insincere at worst. Just some words that could be said as a poor attempt to make the other person feel better. Yet, it's not enough. It's never enough. People say those words because they want the griever to feel better. After all, grief is something bad, and pain is something bad, because feeling grief and pain hurts, yet it is just a natural response to loss.

Who had it worse

The worst part about people trying to be there for grievers is when they share their own grief stories as if this is a competition of who felt worse, who was great at pulling themselves together, and who went back to living their life as if nothing has happened. As if one loss is greater than the other. Indeed, every loss is different, and the grief that accompanies that is just as different, too. There is no comparing the loss of a child to the loss of a grandparent. Yet, both are valid and both completely hurt. It is extremely important to be careful that people's grief is excluded for the sake of others. This sudden competition of whose pain feels worse is the worst way to make the other feel better. The focus would be shifted from being on the griever to the listener and the pain the listener (turned griever now) felt when they lost that special someone. Devine expresses that the listener often feels that an opportunity has come up to talk about their own loss, thinking it will help. However, all it does is steel the focus from the griever, completely negating any help the listener would have been able to give.

Just get over it, will you?

Society does not allow people to grieve properly. People who have experienced loss are just expected to 'get over' what has happened, simply because loss is a part of life, and they're not the first, nor the last people on earth, who have lost loved ones. There is a time and place to share our stories of loss, but it is not when we are trying to comfort another for a loss they've recently experienced. This particular situation is the reason why most people do not actually feel better when they talk about their loss and it's also why most people choose not to share their own feelings of sorrow and pain; the listener forgets that they're trying to help the griever feel better and instead start asking to be comforted in return.

At least you had them for that long

The number of phrases that listeners usually direct to grievers in a poor attempt to make them feel better is just ridiculous. Words like 'you're stronger than you think you are' and 'at least you had them for as long as you did' have an implied, unstated phrase at the end: stop feeling so bad. Stop feeling so bad because your loved one is in a better place now. Stop feeling so bad because you can always have another child/partner. Yes, all that is true, the author says. But saying those words indicate that feeling pain is not okay. Grieving is not okay. Saying those words is just dismissing or diminishing the pain that the griever is feeling, which doesn't really help them feel better. But the worst phrase to be said, Devine says, is 'everything happens for a reason.' As if the person who's just experienced loss and is grieving doesn't actually know that. As if intense loss is the only way to make people more compassionate, selfless, or connected. The author particularly attacks this phrase because she believes that people don't need to lose loved ones to grow, become better individuals, learn to appreciate what they have, or not take things for granted. People can become the best versions of themselves without having to lose their other half, an idol, mentor, parent, or child and then hear words like 'everything happens for a reason'. We know. Everyone knows. The entire planet knows that everything happens for a reason. Instead of saying those words, it is better to help a griever understand that pain is not a problem to be solved, but an experience to be felt and then carried and lived through, which is why the only things a griever needs are support, comfort, and companionship.

Key Takeaway:

The worst thing a griever can do is allow society to dictate how they should feel about loss, or give a chance for other people to demean their pain.

Reflection Questions:

1. Think about the moment the funeral was held and people came over to offer condolences. Did anyone mention any of the phrases explored in this chapter? If yes, how did that make you feel?

———————————————————————————————————

———————————————————————————————————

———————————————————————————————————

———————————————————————————————————

———————————————————————————————————

———————————————————————————————————

———————————————————————————————————

2. After you have experienced that loss, how did people try to comfort you?

_____

_____

_____

_____

_____

_____

3. Think about one person who instead of making you feel better, only made you feel worse. What action or choice of words did that person use that angered you most?

_____

_____

_____

_____

_____

_____

4. Do you believe that the loss you've experienced happened for a reason? If yes, what was it?

_____

_____

_____

_____

_____

_____

5. Do you have anyone in your circle who made your pain and their pain into a competition? How did you feel about that, and how did you react?

_____

_____

_____

_____

_____

_____

Action Step:

Think about the points you read in this chapter. Ask yourself the following questions:

- Should I care if some people had it better/worse?
- How should I deal if some people turn my grief into a competition with theirs?
- Was anyone in my circle trying to fix my pain?
- Am I approaching pain as a problem to be fixed?

Take some time to really ponder these questions and reflect.

Self-Evaluation:

Think about your answers carefully, then compare them to key points in this chapter. Does your perception of pain seem sharper? Is there something you should change about the way you're seeing your own pain? Also write about what conclusion you drew from the action step.

_____

_____

_____

_____

_____

_____

_____

Chapter 3:
It's Not You, It's Us:
Our Models of Grief Are Broken

The thing about grief is we don't how to deal with it once we feel it. When a culture is built upon fairy tales and stories with a happy ending, it's very unlikely that the society can accept a person who's grieving for a long time. How could it be that a person could stay grieving for years? There is an expiration date to everything in this world, but not to grief. To clarify that point, Devine draws a personal example of when she was grieving the loss of her partner, Matt, who drowned on a miserable day. People would express wonder that she 'still' is sad over the loss of her partner a few months after his passing. It is completely frowned upon by culture to grieve for long periods of time, Devine explains. As if grief should be a short-term emotion that disappears after a while, and it's a must to continue life as if loss never happened. Continue by going back to work, attending events, smiling, and in all these situations, the author would meet two kinds of people: those who would ask her to 'just get over it', and others who would only inject her with positivity by expressing how strong, resilient, smart, and beautiful she is, and that her husband loved her so much, and she would still feel his love, but only if she stopped being sad. She would only feel him as if he never left, on the condition that she stops sulking. They mean well, those people, Devine says. She doesn't blame them for saying all those words; they only want to help, their intentions are pure, they don't want to see her sad.

Unfortunately, that's the only way they know how to, yet there's a huge difference between the intentions of those people and how they actually would make her feel.

Seeking professional help only makes it worse

One major problem therapists, psychologists, psychiatrists, and a lot of professionals in the field make is offering two dimensional, often unhelpful advice to those who are grieving, so instead of actually making their patients feel better, they only end up making them feel worse. That's something the author stresses a lot on, especially that all therapists follow Dr. Elisabeth Kubler-Ross's five stages of grief model: denial, anger, bargaining, depression, and acceptance. After feeling grief over the loss of her partner, Devine finally understands why grievers never really benefit much from therapy, and others feel much worse going out of therapy than they did coming in---those stages never really fit.

Grief is unique to us all

There is no one model to explain, understand, or process grief. Everyone feels the loss of a loved one differently, and as such, grieves differently. In fact, it took Dr. Ross years to realize that, where she stated that she regretted breaking grief down into those infamous five stages because they really provided a cage to all grievers: if grievers did not pass through the stages or were not able to move on from them, something was seriously wrong with them. Those stages only made things worse. People who grieve want this roadmap: they want to know what's the right way to grieve and how they can deal with it, but those five stages did more harm than good. Medical professionals, and the lay people, need to respect the pain behind loss, and understand that grief has no rules, no guidebook, and most importantly, that pain is not a condition that needs to be treated. Grief and pain are a part of life, and pain is not this villain that needs to be destroyed by the hero at the end of the movie or book. Pain is very much alive, with an existence in the very throbbing heart of a griever, and being a true hero lies in waking up and facing the day when you'd rather not, understanding that pain is there and it's not going away anytime soon, but it should not be a reason to stop living, or stop loving.

Key Takeaway:

Your pain is entirely your own, and it has no expiration date, so don't let others dictate why and for how long you feel that pain.

Reflection Questions:

1. Think about the first few weeks after your loved one's death. What was people's reaction of your pain?

———————————————————————————————

———————————————————————————————

———————————————————————————————

———————————————————————————————

———————————————————————————————

_____

_____

2. What was your reaction to their comments?

_____

_____

_____

_____

_____

_____

3. Did you seek professional help after your loved one's death? How did that make you feel?

_____

_____

_____

_____

_____

_____

4. What were some ways professional help made you feel better/worse?

_____

_____

_____

_____

_____

_____

_____

5. How long have you grieved for/have been grieving? What do you think contributes to the duration of your grief?

_____

_____

_____

_____

_____

_____

_____

Action Step:

Think about your grief for a second. Do you think you can change something to enhance the way you perceive your grief? Are there ways that can help you understand your grief better? Once you have given some thought into those questions, start to practice them in your daily life. Also, every time someone tries to tell you how you should be feeling, try telling them that solely you own the right to dictate how you should be feeling, and no one has any say over it. Be as candid as you like, and don't sacrifice being firm for the sack of the other's persons feeling.

Self-Evaluation:

Compare your answers to the reflection questions to the content in this chapter. How did this chapter help change your perspective on grief, loss and pain? Also, have you been able to practice telling someone not to tell you how to feel? Take some time to write down your thoughts.

_____

_____

_____

_____

_____

_____

_____

_____

_____

Chapter 4:
Emotional Illiteracy and the Culture of Blame

Devine has a theory that links the judgment a griever is exposed to; to the way they actually respond. She explains how people find it so difficult to accept that a person who is completely healthy might drop dead as they were running on a normal morning. In fact, it is so difficult for them to understand that that they start looking for flaws in the deceased's behavior that led to their doom. The deceased did not work out enough; their diet consisted of unhealthy foods; they shouldn't have been walking on the side of the road that day. As if doing either of that will postpone their death. It's very scary to think that a person could be doing all the right things, wearing the right clothes, taking the necessary vitamins, eating the healthiest food, yet still die. She shares a personal example about how she was blamed by some people for her partner's death because she made him go into the water where he drowned, and then she was judged for the grief she felt even though she was so reserved with her thoughts. Devine uses herself as an example to show that people could be the worst, harshest critiques of others' pain.

It's not your fault

People are so quick to blame grievers for feeling so bad, for not bouncing back to life as if nothing has happened, for not attracting positive thoughts and instead dwelled on the loss they faced. Devine uses Brene

Brown's research to show that people resort to blaming others for not sweeping their pain under the rug and continuing with their lives, because blame is this blanket that protects us from feeling the pain that the other is feeling. If we blamed them for not attracting positive thoughts, we will immediately become disconnected from their pain, so we won't feel the sorrow they do. People don't want to feel that pain because then they would have to imagine that they are to lose someone they hold dear, and the thought is so uncomfortable and unbearable that they immediately say' I can't imagine what you're passing through' to the griever. They don't want to feel that pain, so they directly disconnect themselves from those tragic emotions. This is something people have adopted as a protective mechanism, simply because humans are connected to each other by bonds they don't really see through the limbic system. It's not possible for a person to see another in pain and not feel that pain, which is why that person starts blaming the other for feeling pain, resulting in complete protection against those painful feelings.

Religion and death

It's not possible for a person to talk about death without using religion and God in the same sentence. There are conflicting, contradictory thoughts people have when it comes to both loss and religion. It's so difficult, Devine says, to understand the agenda of a God who chose to save a sick person because their loved ones prayed day and night for them yet allowed for all those global tragedies to exist. It's not possible to conceive why God chooses certain people to live, and others to die,

42

which is why faith is not something that could change the outcome of anything. There's much more to what happens in life or death that we can ever come to understand, which is why using faith to cover feelings of safety, control, and connection is inaccurate at best and unjust at worst, and serves as an extension of our culture of blame.

Staying positive will cure you

The feelings of positivity and induced happiness are another part of this culture that wants to fix pain. Grievers are always asked to stay positive, to rise above the pain, to try to think happy thoughts, because positivity attracts positivity, and there's no way a person could be happy if they are grieving, and a grieving person is an unhealthy person. Worst yet are the traditions that provide explanation as to why loss happened. If that person was kinder/more helpful/less selfish, they wouldn't have died that way. You lost a loved one because it's karma; be kinder to others and you won't face another loss. Suffering will only heal you and help you grow. It's just a lesson life wanted to teach grievers, and they failed at it. She uses the example of Barbara Ehrenreich, an author and researcher who beat cancer with an upbeat attitude, to describe positive thinking as a blanket that means to cover negative emotions, and that poverty, financial distress, losing a loved one, and many other sad situations are advertised as a bliss in disguise. Governments and ruling bodies chose to brainwash the public into believing in thinking positive thoughts. Optimism is a morphine injection meant to dilute the ramifications of poverty, unemployment, inequality, among others. But it doesn't just stop there.

Spirituality, enlightenment, and pain

This culture of running away from pain or hiding it is there in every practice people were taught to do. Spirituality and enlightenment are advertised to help people feel good by helping them cope with pain, when all they do is give people some breathing room in the distress they're feeling, which is not actually the same as making pain go away. Instead of helping grievers cope with pain, spirituality only serves at making people more detached from their feelings, so in a way, it helps them mask the pain rather than live through it. The best way to live through that pain, Devine explains, is by letting it exist, accepting that it's there, that a person is feeling it, not resisting it, and not stopping it in any way. Yes, pain hurts, but it's proof that a person is alive and feeling love and life. There's no true living, and loving, if you cannot feel grief and pain. If a person isn't allowed to grief, or feel pain, they would develop a false sense of control, and they would lead their lives normally, up to a certain point, until everything comes crashing down and they would psychologically collapse or find themselves unable to perform, simply because they did not allow themselves to feel when they should have. Addiction, anxiety, depression, and social isolation are all examples of grief that was not understood, tolerated, and felt.

Pain is acknowledged, but not felt

People have become so desensitized to the pain that exists in the world, the hate crimes, discrimination, wars, and injustices that are there, simply because people have been taught to sweep pain under the rug, to

44

not feel it, to just get over it. People are so scared to feel pain that they'd rather blame others to remove any sort of responsibility they have over that pain. However, there is no chance the world might become a safer, equitable, and more beautiful place for everyone out there if pain is not understood, if people who are grieving continue to be perceived as weak or damaged. To be alive, Devine says, is to feel both love and pain, and to acknowledge that one does not exist without the other, and that even though the latter is very uncomfortable and hurts to feel, people should not lie to themselves by telling themselves they feel good when they don't; pain should be given a place on the table, right next to love, not swept under the rug.

Key Takeaway:

The world will blame everyone for the loss that happened, but itself. Pain will never be understood and dealt with using the right attitude when people choose to shy away from pain than accept that it's a natural part of life.

Reflection Questions:

1. Thinking about the loss you've experienced, did you ever come across a situation where people were unfair to you in their reactions? How so?

_____

_____

_____

_____

_____

_____

_____

2. What, in your opinion, is the relationship between having positive thoughts, and the way you're dealing with loss?

_____

_____

_____

_____

_____

_____

3. How did religion affect the way you perceived the death of your loved one?

_____

_____

_____

_____

_____

_____

4. Have spirituality and enlightenment been a part of your life before death? If yes, did they alter your perception of how grief should be dealt with?

_____

_____

_____

_____

_____

_____

_____

5. What do you think should change in the world for people to perceive grievers differently?

_____

_____

_____

_____

_____

_____

_____

Action Step:

Accept the pain you are feeling by validating it. Give that pain a body, and respect it. When someone tries to tell you how to feel or was unfair to you, tell them that you understand your own pain, and encourage them to accept it. Your approach to pain should be open. The world shuns pain enough and that's why it won't accept or validate your pain or others'.

Self-Evaluation:

Are there ways you believe should change in how you deal with pain, having read this chapter? How has the action step progressed for you over the last week?

_____

_____

_____

_____

_____

_____

_____

_____

_____

_____

_____

Chapter 5:
The New Model of Grief

Devine mentions that people usually deal with grief in two ways only: either they are stuck in grief, immobilized by their own pain, or they come out of grief a transformed and enlightened human being. Black or white, no shades of gray in between, that's how society grieves, but it cannot be more unjust to grievers to fail to recognize that a whole world lies in the color of gray, simply because it's not possible to continue living in eternal grief, but it is also equally impossible to become a chirpier, happier person after going down that tunnel of pain. It's a work in progress, one that sees the griever slowly becoming more courageous to open those blinds and peak into life back again after witnessing that crippling loss. Yet, it shouldn't be rushed. Obsessing over the idea of ending grief to go back to normal is just bottling grief inside and not airing it out. Rushing through grief and not understanding it or feeling it the way a person should; can halt any progress a person may have for any future connection or intimacy with others.

Don't fix grief, understand it

Grief is always looked at as if it's a problem to be solved. Love is not a problem to be solved, so why should grief? Why should any feeling or emotion be regarded as a problem to be solved, when it should be understood and incorporated into your life? If people were to fully embrace the pain, the heartache, and the hurt of loss, life would not necessarily have less grief in it, but it would certainly be more beautiful. When culture, people, friends, family members, books, and even societal responses learn to perceive grief as an emotion just like any other and be kind and empathetic towards it, there might be a way to change the world. Getting through the pain of loss can only happen when that pain is felt, shared, and expressed by those around the griever. So rather than being worried that another's pain would rub off on the listener, people should understand that the griever's pain would only serve to connect them to each other.

Key Takeaway:

Grief, just like love, speaks many languages and can serve to unify people everywhere around the world.

Reflection Questions:

1. Do you feel more connected to your grief when you share your pain with others? In what way?

_____

_____

_____

_____

_____

_____

_____

2. Do you believe that pain can unify people? How so?

_____

_____

_____

_____

_____

_____

3. Where do you find yourself now, on which end of the spectrum? Are you closer to the white, or black part?

_____

_____

_____

_____

_____

_____

4. What, in your opinion, can help you move along the process of accepting pain? How can you adopt that?

_____

_____

_____

_____

_____

_____

_____

5. In what ways should the world change, in your opinion, to make it a more accepting place for pain?

_____

_____

_____

_____

_____

_____

_____

Action Step:

Because getting though the pain of loss can only happen when that pain is felt, shared, and expressed by those around you, take some time to find a way to connect with the people in your life. Also, think about a time when someone you love lost a special person. What was your reaction to their grief and in what ways do you believe you can relate to them? Understand them? Do you agree that pain might help you connect with that person? Whether you are the griever or the listener, find a way to connect with others through pain.

Self-Evaluation:

How did your perception of grief and pain change after reading this chapter and answering the reflection questions? Have you been able to make a connection with at least one person though shared pain?

_____

_____

_____

_____

_____

_____

_____

_____

_____

_____

_____

_____

_____

_____

_____

Are you enjoying the book so far?

If so, please help us reach more readers by taking 30 seconds to write just a few words on Amazon by using the QR code below

Or, you can choose to leave one later...

Scan me

Part II
What to Do with Your Grief

Chapter 6:
Living in the Reality of Loss

When a person has lost a loved one, they tend to go deep into themselves. They go very deep into that space where no one can reach them, and that's okay. A griever has just loss someone incredibly important to them, and they are allowed to be given that respite. The author of this book is gently asking for entry into that dark space. She does not aim to remove that griever from the darkness they are in, but she wants to tell them it's okay that they are there. They can come out whenever they feel ready. It's okay to feel rage. It's okay to ask, 'why me, why now'. All those feelings that come after loss are completely normal to be felt. Right now, the pain is so bad. Life just seems bleak, and a griever has the right to be angry at losing that loved one, even though their culture doesn't accept it.

When is it the right time?

Sometimes, things need to be dealt with, like burials, farewell ceremonies, choosing the right casket, if cremation is to happen or not, among others. At times, it's absolutely difficult to deal with that, and a griever would have to put on this mask of 'I'm fine' when they're really slowly dying inside. Sometimes, they want to go through all that as a tribute to the lost one, making these rituals the only way to say goodbye. Other times, the whole process is too overwhelming and they don't want to do it, so they delegate these tasks to family members and close ones.

It's not just you who are grieving, your kids are too

Devine mentions that her partner had a son who turned 18 one day after the partner's death. He chose to not disclose any of the feelings he felt at the time. Even though he did not let Devine in to help process Matt's death together, they did talk around the topic of death and lightly on how it is affecting them. She states that she doesn't have experience dealing with grieving children since she herself had no kids with Matt, so she mentions an agency that can help a griever navigate loss within a family, and that's Dougy center in Oregon.

Anniversaries, Events, and Birthdays

There is no right way to break this down, so we'll just go ahead and say it. Loss is overwhelming, and grief can be crippling. Having your loved one's birthday come when they're not actually there only serves to remind you that you've lost them forever, but that doesn't mean that their memory doesn't still live through you. The author talks about how difficult it was for her to join in events that commemorate her partner's life, especially when her own mother and his mother were doing the planning. She stresses that sometimes the wounds are too fresh, and she urges the griever to do what they think is best. The griever can leave the event, even if they just got there, even if they were in on the planning. Let the griever do them, without caring about what others might think. No one feels what they're going through, anyway.

When to redecorate, and when to let go of your lost one's belongings

Devine refers to a vomit metric. It technically means that if giving away the lost one's wardrobe, redecorating their room, or spreading their ashes make the bile in your throat rise, don't. Take as long as you need to process the loss that has happened. Don't change anything, whatsoever, if it makes you feel like vomiting. Once thinking about doing any of those doesn't trigger that reflex, you're in a safe space and can go ahead and do what needs to be done. She, herself, didn't change the sheets she and Matt slept on until a year later. The tub of ice cream her partner ate from last moved with her to two consecutive houses, where she was only able to let go of it four years after her partner's death.

Shopping, friends, and disappointments

Driving one hour to go to a different grocery store to avoid seeing a friend, acquaintance, or family member is completely okay. People can ask intrusive questions that a griever might just not be ready to answer. Going out of their own way to shop at different places is normal. Avoiding probing questions is normal. The loss that has happened still did not get processed yet. The grief that came along with it needs a long way to go, maybe not even ever. Questions like 'when are you getting married again', and 'are you giving away the deceased's clothes' are insensitive at best. The griever can refrain from answering them. But what's worse, Devine says, is the disappearance of the so-called friends whose support was so much needed, yet nowhere to be found, after a person loses a loved one. It just adds more to the pain, and it's an injustice in and of itself.

Key Takeaway:

There is no right way to grief, no right time to donate or remove the lost one's belongings, and no right anything. What is right for a griever will not be for others, and that's alright.

Reflection Questions:

1. Think about the funeral arrangements of your loved ones. Did you take care of that, or someone else did? Why is that?

_____

_____

_____

_____

_____

_____

_____

2. Do you believe that there is a right time to say good-bye to your loved one's belongings? What factors determine that?

_____

_____

_____

_____

_____

_____

_____

3. In a world that doesn't accept grief, how did events and birthdays belonging to your lost one go?

_____

_____

_____

_____

_____

_____

4. Are there any children that were affected by the lost one's death? If yes, how did they react?

_____

_____

_____

_____

_____

_____

_____

5. If there were children involved, how did grief affect them? Your relationship with them?

_____

_____

_____

_____

_____

_____

_____

Action Step:

Monitor your own reactions to events and birthdays belonging to your loved one. How did they change over time? What are some ways you feel this chapter has helped in? Are there points you agree or disagree with found in this chapter? Think about those for a minute and reflect on your answers.

Self-Evaluation:

Compare your answers to the self-reflection questions to what you have learned in this chapter. Write down major points you feel will help you with future events.

Chapter 7:
You Can't Solve Grief,
but You Don't Have to Suffer

In previous chapters, we talked about how society views pain and grief as problems to be solved as opposed to emotions to be experienced. This is something that the author stresses on here. So, if pain and grief shouldn't be perceived as problems that need solutions, how can we alleviate them? How can we carry on living with this stab wound in our hearts? In order to answer those questions, it's crucial to understand that there's a difference between pain, and suffering. Pain, we cannot solve, but suffering, we can fix. The author proposes a few techniques that she herself has practiced, and those techniques proved helpful.

Pain versus suffering

Pain is a normal, healthy response people feel when they experience a loss. It feels bad to experience pain, but that doesn't make it wrong. Suffering, on the other hand, is felt when people feel dismissed, unsupported, neglected, or abnormal because they're feeling pain. It's the byproduct of others judging your pain, or an experience felt when you starve your body of food, sleep, comfort, or its basic needs. Suffering has some friends, and these include anxiety, fear, and isolation. This is why suffering will always be much worse than feeling pain, simply because it's a party of negativity and negative emotions.

How to reduce suffering

- Understand that what used to give comfort before, now might have a completely opposing effect. This can include words of comfort, certain activities, simple gestures, anything, really.

- Understand that the body responds to both external and internal stimuli. Our bodies were designed to express love, pain, hurt, and a wide array of different emotions, so allow your body to express pain, because bottling it inside will only lead to unresolved, unfixable issues down the road and in the near future.

- Don't try to heal your own pain. Learn to live through it by taking things one step at a time. Learn what makes you 'tick' by experimenting with pain. Sometimes, a certain smell might make you erupt. Maybe a specific activity, like taking a walk before bed, can make you sleep better. Learn what activities make things better or worse, and then make a note of that in a journal, on your phone, anywhere.

- Don't focus on removing pain, instead, do what you can to reduce suffering. Tend to your grief without feeling like you should fix it. Don't approach your pain with the intent of making it disappear, or less pronounced. Use that approach to fix suffering.

Your loss is not a test

The author emphasizes this throughout her book. When a person loses a loved one, the first thing they hear from everyone around them is that this is a test, and they should be strong enough to pass it. Grief is not a test, and it will never be. It's an experiment in love. Grief can show you how to experiment with yourself, your life, your family, and future relationships, by helping you understand what you can and cannot accept after a particular loss. Your ability to carry that pain with you as you go about doing your daily routine, knowing that your loved one will never come back, communicates strength. Figuring out how you can survive the next minute, and the next five, knowing that you've lost that person, all determine your strength. Everyone has experienced loss in the past, and they will continue to do so in the future, but everyone grieves in a different way, and each person's grief is completely their own, just as their love is.

Turning toxic thoughts into healthy ones

The griever will always be bombarded by plaguing thoughts of things they could've done differently. Signs that they missed, indicators that they were blind to, how they can proceed on with life from there knowing that things will never be the same again. All these thoughts create suffering. They make things worse, much worse than they actually are, and they need to be banished. They must be replaced by wellness thoughts, where the griever would acknowledge that they're feeling pain, but they're calm about it. They understand that the more they accept pain, the better they can live with it. Differentiating between worseness thoughts and wellness thoughts can help the griever understand the connection between certain thoughts and how these can make them feel. When the griever understands that worseness thoughts will only increase suffering, they can learn to steer their mind away from such thoughts and instead focus on less painful ones. That is extremely helpful to a griever who is so lost in pain that they become a victim to their own thoughts.

Key Takeaway:

Approaching grief with a mindset of fixing will never work, simply because grief is not a problem to be fixed, but an experience to be lived.

Reflection Questions:

1. Have you ever looked at grief in a solution-oriented way? Does everyone around you want to fix your pain? Why do you think that is?

_____

_____

_____

_____

_____

_____

_____

2. Have you made yourself suffer during pain? Did you tend to yourself and body? How did that happen?

_____

_____

_____

_____

_____

_____

_____

3. Having read this chapter, what are helpful ways to fix your suffering?

_____

_____

_____

_____

_____

_____

_____

4. Have you ever been told that what you're passing through is a test? After reading this chapter, do you still have the same view or hold a different one? Why?

_____

_____

_____

_____

_____

_____

_____

5. What are some ways you can explore that will help you turn your thoughts from worseness ones to wellness ones?

_____

_____

_____

_____

_____

_____

_____

Action Step:

Keep a journal of your feelings throughout the day. Divide your journal into two parts. One will be for suffering signs, and the other will be for wellness signs. Signs that you're taking care of yourself. Think about why they would be considered suffering or wellness signs. Think of ways you can banish worseness thoughts from your mind. Explore ways to increase the frequency of wellness thoughts, and ask yourself what might bring them on. Can certain activities trigger them?

Self-Evaluation:

Write down how you have been doing with the main theme of chapter 7. Have you been able to distinguish between wellness and worseness thoughts?

_____

_____

_____

_____

_____

_____

_____

_____

_____

Chapter 8:
How (and Why) to Stay Alive

It's so hard to understand that you need to continue living when your loved one is not there to experience life with you. Worse yet, that you are still alive and must continue living when they are not there to share that life with you. In fact, these feelings give birth to even more dangerous, but completely normal thoughts.

Grief and suicide

Waking up the next day, knowing that your loved one is not there to live it with you, seems like a very unfortunate thing. 'Oh, God. I woke up today, why did I have to wake up? Why couldn't I just die?' you'll ask yourself. Thoughts about not wanting to be alive raid your mind, and they are okay. They're not to be confused with thoughts of wanting to hurt yourself. Not wanting to be alive and wanting to kill yourself are not the same, and if you feel like doing yourself harm, please reach out for professional help. Others have been there before and getting specialized help will help you deal with those emotions.

Surviving pain

It's simply not possible to talk about pain without referring to the Buddha who taught people Upekkha. Upekkha entails staying open to pain and experiencing it, remaining calm in the face of pain even though you know there's not one thing you can change about what has happened. It's the most difficult teaching to practice because it involves a person standing witness to the pain, staring it in the eye, and surviving it. Pain is so loud. It's there and it's not going away anytime soon when it's brought about by the loss of a loved one. It's so big that people in pain often seek natural landscapes that are so wide and large, much bigger than the pain they're feeling. People believe that by staring at the horizon line, by talking to the waves, some of the pain will wash away, and it does sometimes. Other times, it doesn't, to which it's important to simply come to pain with open eyes and an open heart. Trust yourself, Mirabai encourages, to be able to handle the pain that you're in. Care for yourself when you're in pain, because the world is cruel as is, and you don't deserve more cruelty than what was served to you when you lost that person you hold dear.

Be there for your pain, and don't try to find your happy place

Devine talks about one of the worst memories she had when she was just learning to accept her pain, and that was on an unfortunate day: Valentine's Day. She didn't know it was Valentine's at the time, and she was going into a store to shop for a few items when she was bombarded by the sight of couples everywhere. Couples that had their loved ones with them, when she didn't have her Matt. Couples who will lose their partners sometime in the future, just like she did her Matt. It was so difficult for her to stay there in the store. She rushed back to her car and after several attempts at trying to reach her support system but failing,

78

she focused on her environment. She tried to ground herself by focusing on and counting all things orange. It would have been so easy for her, she mentions, to just drive herself into an accident, but she didn't want to create another widow, or widower, for that matter. So, she practiced what she would often instruct her clients to do when they're overwhelmed by the grief they are feeling, and it worked. Focusing on something mundane and ordinary helped her, for a few moments, replace that pain when it grew too big, and doing that helped her. It might help you too.

Self-care

It's so hard to be kind to yourself when you're here and they're not. But remember, you are not alone in this world. Not caring for yourself will backfire on you, but most importantly (because you don't really care about yourself at the moment, and might not for a long time), on your loved ones. Do you really want those in your life who love you to go through that same pain that you are going through if they had to lose you? Do you want to bring upon them this kind of grief? You alone can answer those questions, but in a world brimming with cruelty, adding more pain when it's unnecessary might just not be the answer. Practice self-care, eat to keep your body sustained, even if you don't feel like it, and always, always, be kind to yourself. The author built a connection with another widow and they both promised each other to not harm themselves, because they wouldn't want to cause the other pain. They promised to take care of their own bodies, because the world is a painful place to be in already. Losing a loved one, as you have experienced, is not the easiest thing in the world. Maybe not everyone can be as fortunate (if fortunate can even be used in this book), but we all need a safe haven, either in the form of a place, thing, or person.

Key Takeaway:

Be kind to yourself and take care of it even when you don't want to, because not fixing suffering will only add more pain to what you're already experiencing.

Reflection Questions:

1. When your loss happened, how were you able to take care of yourself?

_____

_____

_____

_____

_____

_____

_____

2. Did you have anyone in your life currently or at the time to help you take care of yourself? If yes, how so, and if not, how did you deal?

_____

_____

_____

_____

_____

_____

_____

3. Did you feel at times that you don't wish to live? How did you cope with those feelings?

_____

_____

_____

_____

_____

_____

4. How did you process thoughts about your grief at the time?

_____

_____

_____

_____

_____

_____

_____

5. In what ways did this chapter help you?

_____

_____

_____

_____

_____

_____

_____

Action Step:

In your journal, write down the following:

1. I deserve to live even though my loved one is not here with me anymore.

2. There is a purpose to my life, even if I don't know it yet, even if I'll never truly know it.

3. I don't want to bring people I care about the same pain I am experiencing.

4. I will take care of myself by sustaining my body with food, sleep, and time off as much as possible.

Self-Evaluation:

How are you doing with the main themes of this chapter? How are you doing with the action step? Write down your thoughts and feeling about chapter 8.

_____

_____

_____

_____

_____

_____

_____

_____

_____

_____

_____

_____

_____

_____

_____

_____

_____

Chapter 9:
What Happened to My Mind?
Dealing with Grief's Physical Side Effects

One side effect that grief has is the fact that it disturbs your sleep cycle. You will find yourself too often either not sleeping well or sleeping too much, waking up in the middle of the night or going to sleep at 10 in the morning. You might find yourself waking up right at the time your loved one used to; it's all normal. You might not even fall asleep easily or get any much sleep during the first few weeks. Just try to rest when you can, and understand that what has happened affected and will continue to affect the way your body works. Sometimes, falling asleep is the worst thing you can do. That's when your demons come out to play and the nightmares start rolling. Dreams are the mind's natural way of expressing itself, so don't try to overanalyze it or repress it. Let your unconscious mind have a safe space for it to get to terms with pain, just like your conscious mind does.

Grief and the body

Our bodies are almost always communicating with us, but we don't often give them the time of the day. However, when we lose a loved one, these phantom pains start appearing in different parts of our body. We start developing the body aches that our loved ones used to complain of. It's completely possible to start having heartburns, develop respiratory or cardiac problems, chest pains, loss of appetite, and plenty more. Eating too little or too much is something you might experience upon the loss of a loved one. Other health issues might arise, like diabetes, high blood pressure, high levels of blood cholesterol, etc. Losing weight or gaining weight are completely plausible at this time. When you couldn't care less about what happens to yourself or body, remember to be kind to yourself and sustain it. There's a reason why you're still here, on this planet, in this cruel world.

Grief and the brain

For a while after the death of a loved one, a person will feel like they're losing their mind. The griever will at times place frozen goods in the washing machine instead of the freezer. Keys will go into bathroom cupboards instead of the living room dresser. Appointments will be missed, people's names will slip by, and plenty of other situations that a previously sharp mind never had a problem with. A person becomes a vegetable, sort to speak. That's what grief made them out to be. There used to be a certain capacity to what the brain could do, but grief affected it so negatively that now running the most mundane errand or remembering the silliest thing is the most difficult thing in the world. Keep reminders, the author advises. Fill the entire house with post-its and notes if that's what it takes, and learn to go easy on your brain. It's also grieving.

What day is it?

A question you'll find yourself asking all the time. A griever is someone who loses track of time. Days become a blur, weeks just pass by, and sometimes even years seem like days when a loved one is lost forever. It makes complete sense for the mind to be in a fog, but allowing lost time to be instead of fighting it will make things easier. A voracious reader who is experiencing grief might abhor the very sight of a few lines. It might take a few tries to actually comprehend what's being said. That's normal. It will take time for reading abilities to be restored, and it just might never go back to normal. The world will become a bizarre and confusing place, where returning change to the cashier will seem like solving differential equations. Forgetting where things were placed is the new norm, and even the slightest social interactions seem like rocket science. These feelings are completely normal, and the worst thing you can do is compare what you are now to who you were before. You are not the same person you were, pre-loss. However, eventually, the brain will create new pathways around that grief. It will seem like forever before you remember that house keys do not belong in the bathroom, but you will get there. Because the brain is this insanely resilient organ that can arrange itself around the pain, while acknowledging it's there all the same. This might take months, or it might take years, but the good news is you'll eventually get there.

Key Takeaway:

Grief will affect the body, brain, and your entire life. Accept that everything in you will change as a result of grief, and that's completely normal.

Reflection Questions:

1. During the time when you were, are grieving, what are some ways your behavior changed?

_____

_____

_____

_____

_____

_____

2. What's a crazy place you've placed your keys/ IDs/ important belonging in?

_____

_____

_____

_____

_____

_____

_____

3. How do you feel grief affected your mind? Your body?

_____

_____

_____

_____

_____

_____

4. Are there any days when you felt you don't remember the date? Do you still have that? How did you cope with it?

_____

_____

_____

_____

_____

_____

5. Did you have any nightmares after you lost your loved one? If so, describe them. How did you deal with them the next morning and throughout the day?

_____

_____

_____

_____

_____

_____

_____

Action Step:

Tell yourself the following every day this week.

1. I accept that grief affected my body and brain.

2. I know that my behavior and attitude toward certain things have changed, and that's okay.

3. I will put post-its or other notes to remind me of important events, dates, meeting times, and other things.

4. I can dabble into practicing mind-sharpening games in order to get my mind more focused.

5. I will pay attention to how my focus has changed due to pain, and I will accept my abilities regardless.

Self-Evaluation:

Explore this chapter's main theme of your body being affected by grief. Have you been able to accept the changes that have occurred both to your mind and body?

_____

_____

_____

_____

_____

_____

_____

_____

_____

_____

_____

_____

_____

_____

_____

_____

_____

Chapter 10:
Grief and Anxiety:
Calming Your Mind When
Logic Doesn't Work

Losing a loved one brings out all buried demons to play, especially the worst one: anxiety. There is no saying what anxiety might do to a griever, but it certainly isn't happiness, rainbows and sunshine. Anxiety manifests itself as fear that something will happen. The griever would be bombarded by incessant thoughts of their pet running away and dying of cold or a drunk driver, or leaving the stove on and the house burning down, and plenty of similar scenarios. It's how our brains function. Brains are very good at what they do. They help us imagine situations so that we are extra careful not to actually live them. That's why the thoughts our brains conjure are the most dangerous weapons against us. We imagine multiple potential disasters, adding more fuel to the already deranged mind that's controlling our thought process. However, we fail to realize that in the process of keeping ourselves safe against all those dangers, we're pushing our brains to exhaustion. We think that our anxiety is keeping us safe, when the only thing it's doing is providing a false sense of security. Calling other loved ones every minute of the day does not guarantee that they'll remain safe after the minute you hang up. It's a vicious cycle.

How to deal with anxiety on the short and long run

- Anxiety is the accumulation of fear. It's not a guarantee that something will or will not happen. Trying to suppress it will only make it worse. Accept that you're facing anxiety and it's blaring full on.

- Anxiety comes from the fact that you feel something is going to happen and you won't have any control over it. There's one thing only you can control, though, and that's your breathing. Make your exhales longer than your inhales, even if just for fractions of a second longer. Doing so will create an onset of soothing reactions in the body, and it will help calm you down.

- If your anxiety is connected to how you're feeling physically or emotionally, note any changes in your feelings and respond accordingly. Sleep, rest, eat, or move. Care for yourself and address those physical needs. It can reduce your anxiety by a long shot.

- Don't investigate why you're feeling anxious. Expend energy on trying to maintain a calm rather than understanding why anxiety is hitting full force. You'll focus on that later when the attack isn't as strong.

- Learn to trust yourself, replace disaster scenarios with positive images, and find a neutral place for yourself where neither anxiety defeats you nor you defeat it-- you'll just find a middle ground and stay there for a while. Trust that in case something bad happens, you can deal with it. It's tricky, but there's no going around this bit. Knowing that you can handle whatever comes your way can destroy your fears instead of their holding you captive.

- Know that you didn't create your own reality. It's not your fault that your loved one is not with you. Your mind will keep giving you reasons to blame yourself, but if there was something you could have done, physically, emotionally, spiritually, you would have done it without thought. Unlike what the false gurus of today's society say, your thoughts are not your reality. If they were, accidents wouldn't happen, illnesses would disappear, everyone would get ridiculously rich. But that's not our society right now, is it?

- Your mind is the smartest organ on you. Use it to create beautiful images and positive scenarios. Let your mind run on super power to find neutral ground between you and your anxiety. At any moment, tell yourself that you're not safe, but not in danger, either. Create a space of alert calm, where you're neither rehearsing disaster nor falling back into denial over life's risks. You're not above, but not below anything, either. Don't allow your mind to create a future you don't want.

- Acknowledge that you feel anxiety, that you're scared, that you don't trust the world. Do not hide or bottle your feelings for fear of being perceived as fragile or weak in front of others. Ask for comfort when you need it, ask for more information about a situation before venturing into it, and be kind to yourself. If you feel like you need to go back home to check on your pets or kids and you're completely scared something has happened to them, it's entirely okay to go and check on them. Sometimes, being kind to yourself constitute listening to what your anxious brain is telling you and then doing what it tells you to do. That's normal. Don't block it.

Key Takeaway:

Grief has a way of making anxiety run on full blast, making us believe things that aren't there or create scenarios in our minds.

Reflection Questions:

1. Has anxiety always been a part of your life, or did you recently develop it?

_____

_____

_____

_____

_____

_____

_____

2. How do you deal with your anxiety?

_____

_____

_____

_____

_____

_____

_____

3. Is your anxiety triggered by certain scenarios? What are they?

_____

_____

_____

_____

_____

_____

_____

4. Are there certain things that put your anxiety to sleep? What are they?

_____

_____

_____

_____

_____

_____

_____

5. Do you treat your anxiety as something to be ashamed of or as something that needs to be dealt with?

_____

_____

_____

_____

_____

_____

_____

Action Step:

Read the bullet points in this chapter, and next to each, write down your own opinion and thoughts about it. Then, without overwhelming yourself, choose a couple of bullet points and commit to practicing that bullet point daily.

Self-Evaluation:

Have you been able to practice at least one of the bullet points in this chapter? If so, has it made a difference? If not, then write about why you think it hasn't. Then write your own thoughts about the main theme of chapter 10.

_____

_____

_____

_____

_____

_____

_____

_____

_____

_____

_____

_____

_____

_____

_____

_____

_____

Chapter 11:
What Does Art Have to Do with Anything

Grief is a monster living inside us, one that seems to be an eternal companion the minute we lose a loved one. Caging it deep inside only makes it more frustrated, so it lashes out and hurts us even more. Its sharp talons dig deeper into the flesh of our hearts, thereby making us bleed, and hurt even more. That's why it's incredibly important to unleash that grief in healthy ways. Give it the freedom it seeks in any creative form. Doing so might not always be enough for that grief. Being creative will not always dull the pain that grief is associated with, but it's the healthiest form of expressing that grief.

Art and grief

As humans, we need to create something to feel alive. Whether it's a piece of writing, music, or a drawing, the need to create is a part of human nature. A person in grief might resort to being creative as a way to live through the pain. However, it might not necessarily instantaneously make a griever feel better. This goes completely against what our culture thinks: creativity can help grief dim, or destroy it altogether. That couldn't be farther from the truth. Being creative or producing art will not solve anything or make things right. Yet, pain needs expression. We were built in a way where our mind goes instantly to creative expression when it's feeling, especially when we're living in a world that doesn't want to hear our pain, or just wants to fix it.

A canvas will never judge a griever for their pain. A writing pad will never be 'not in the mood' to listen to the heartache and loss. It certainly wouldn't mind the tears that would drop on it when a certain memory comes to mind. Creation allows a griever to connect to the world again because creating something will embody that grief in its very form. The most famous works of art, be it sculptures, paintings, drawings, or poetry, only came to existence because their producers were experiencing tremendous pain at the time. Pain that this world will never understand.

Writing and grief

A griever who used to be a writer, or was a lover of writing or the written word, might abhor the sight of words, just like the author did. However, recent studies have shown that writing for as little as ten minutes a day can lower the levels of cortisol, the stress hormone in the body, significantly. Writing will not bring the deceased back, nor will it really solve anything, nor can it promise anything. At times, the words can just leak out of the writer and there's no stopping that, very much like Rumi's poetry did upon loss of his beloved life-long companion, Shams of Tabriz. Writing should not always be beautiful. It can be the ugly, profane, crazy, but it's still very uniquely the griever's. Devine set up writing classes for grievers, and the first thing she promised them was writing might not help them feel better. She asked them to delve fully into their pain; nothing is off-limits. She asked them to open those gates that are repressing that pain. The only way to heal from pain is to live through it, to know that it exists and it's staying for a while, but they should be able to live with it, anyway. She recommended creating a character out of

102

grief, where it has a physical form and a voice, and communicating with it.

Graphic novels, collages, photography, and many others

Sometimes, words can fail us. It might not be possible for us to put into words the pain we are feeling, which is why resorting to different art forms can help. Graphic novels are an art form many have chosen to resort to. They'd make their loved ones the hero of the story, or create a character out of the grief they were facing. That's what Tom Hart did on the sudden death of his two-year old daughter, Rosalie. If the idea doesn't seem too appealing, maintaining a sketch book with pictures and gesture drawings, or creating collages, can work just fine. Devine would create collages out of discarded magazines, picking pictures randomly because they spoke to her, and then she'd glue them on thick cardboard. Fellow widows found solace in photography, while others poured their pain out in cooking different dishes. Some chose sculpting, where the sculpture would be the very embodiment of that pain. It doesn't matter what art form the griever chooses to resort to. What's most important is that there's no need to produce a perfect piece. There's the griever and their pain, and it's their story to tell, whether through poetry, writing, or any other form of expression.

Key Takeaway:

Creativity is the healthiest way to communicate grief. It can constitute creating different forms of art, writing, photography, cooking, or sculpting.

Reflection Questions:

1. Were you a producer of creative works prior to the loss of your loved one? If yes, what did you create?

_____

_____

_____

_____

_____

_____

2. How has losing a loved one change your creativity levels?

_____

_____

_____

_____

_____

_____

3. What are ways you are comfortable with that will help you channel your pain creatively?

_____

_____

_____

_____

_____

_____

_____

4. Are there any forms of creativity that you would like to try to help ease the pain of your loss? What are they?

_____

_____

_____

_____

_____

_____

_____

5. If you have resorted to any of the creative forms of expressing pain mentioned in this chapter, or have continued to create in your chosen medium, how did that help you cope with grief?

_____

_____

_____

_____

_____

_____

_____

Action Step:

Find out ways in which you can express your grief healthily. Feel free to choose any of the ways mentioned in this chapter, and if not mentioned, feel free to explore other options as well. Try something you never experienced or done before your grief. Monitor how that makes you feel. Be open-minded. You might like things you never thought you would before. Accept that what used to make you happy or entertained might not anymore.

Self-Evaluation:

What experience did you decide to try? Has it been a good experience, or have you found it hard to do?

_____

_____

_____

_____

_____

_____

_____

_____

_____

_____

_____

_____

_____

_____

_____

_____

_____

Chapter 12:
Find Your Own Image of Recovery

What a griever has passed through is not something that could be put in words, per se. The pain is too intense, the feelings too raw, that a person in grief will think that this is how their life will be until their time comes. Talking to a person who's grieving is like walking on egg shells, and using words like hope and recovery might just diffuse the emotional bomb they have inside them. However, life is not one worth living when choosing the right words to say to a griever is deemed an impossible task.

Hope and recovery: be careful with those words

The language that's used around a griever must be chosen with utmost care and precision. If you ask a griever to have hope, specify in what, exactly. But at no point in time will a griever respond positively to words like ' hope that it will get better'. What exactly, might get better, when they have lost their loved one forever? Telling a griever that they'll recover from that loss is like stabbing them in the heart. How can a person recover from a loss that will transform the very fabric of their existence, their very DNA, their entire lives? Even the body and brain change with grief. Things will never get back to normal. Instead, a new normal will have to be created, one that will be without the griever's loved one. Telling a griever that they will recover, the author says, is like telling someone who lost their legs that they'll grow another pair. Absurd, isn't it?

There's no moving on, but is there any getting better?

Returning to normal, and moving on, are not two things feasible for a griever. A griever will not go back to normal, back to the routine they had established prior to the loss; they'll not even return to being the same people they were. Grief is such an intense, life-changing experience that going into it will completely transform a person. Researcher and author Samira Thomas expresses that there are certain things in life that cause people to cross a threshold that changes them forever. People will, upon first experiencing grief, be hurt and broken. At the beginning, they'll lose all shape and form, and asking them to move on is an impossible request. Instead, telling the griever to listen to their wounds, to be honest about the state of their own devastation, to have patience in knowing that grief will forever change them, is more likely to help them live through their pain. It's so difficult for the griever to accept that they have the right to continue living even though their loved one ceased to exist. Grievers have the right to laugh and feel bursts of happiness upon hearing or watching something. It doesn't make their grief any less visible, or their connection or love to their lost one less strong. There's a huge difference between the pain of losing that person. The love the griever holds for that person. They're connected, but they're not the same. The pain will eventually recede, but love will never do. Moving forward in this life does not mean that the love for that person is not there, or that connection to that person has faded. As the griever moves forward in this life, so will all their emotions. As Devine says: ' Recovery in grief is a process of moving with what was, what might have been, and what still remains.'

What hope and recovery look like for a griever

A griever has absolute control over their life, even if the entire world has an opinion over how a griever should be feeling at any given time and what they should be doing after losing that person. Devine tells the griever that only they can choose how to grieve, what to feel, and where to go next in life. She tells the griever to trust that the way they choose to live their life is under their control. She advises the griever to stay true to themselves and hold fiercely to their own hearts. She asks the griever to give themselves an image, a goal, something to look forward to, to hope to accomplish, and to honor their own choice of how they wish to live their lives after that loss happened.

Key Takeaway:

Grief will change a person, so they become different people after experiencing loss, and even though the world will judge the griever for becoming another person, the griever should focus on constructing a new life for themselves where grief will be a companion.

Reflection Questions:

1. Think about the person you were before and after your loss. In what ways have you stayed the same?

_____

_____

_____

2. In what ways did experiencing loss make you a different person?

_____

_____

_____

_____

_____

_____

3. How often do you laugh? What contributes to that?

_____

_____

_____

_____

_____

4. Is there anything currently in your life that makes you look forward to forging a new life?

_____

_____

_____

_____

_____

_____

_____

_____

5. What are some words or actions that soothe you? What are some that anger of frustrate you?

_____

_____

_____

_____

_____

_____

_____

Action Step:

Tell yourself the following every day this week:
- - I know what was taken will never be returned.
- - I deserve to be happy even if it will take a while.
- - My body deserves my attention and care.
- - I must be kind to myself.
- - I will take care of myself.
- - I will be the person I want to be. I deserve it.

Self-Evaluation:

As you go about your day, have you taken notice of things that before didn't matter much, but now have become something that now influences your new life? Did watching something specific, or reading something specific, affect the way you perceive your life after the loss of a loved one, or direct it in any way?

_____

_____

_____

_____

_____

_____

_____

Part III
When Friends and Family
Don't Know What to Do

Chapter 13:
Should You Educate or Ignore Them?

Being in grief will be the loneliest time in your life as a griever, and that's not necessarily a bad thing. The author shares how when her partner first died, she shared the details of her loss with everyone who asked. It only made her feel worse. Sharing grief with other people is sometimes such an intimate act that only a select few deserve to live it with you. People are incredibly curious, and Devine divides them into two categories. The first includes those who will ask probing questions, provide unhelpful support, dismiss and try to cheer you up for you to get over it. The other includes those who so badly want to help, provide you with love and support, but whatever they're doing is not helping. Feel free to drop the first category entirely by setting clear boundaries of what you wish and don't wish to communicate about, and be clear with the second about what they are doing that isn't helping.

Be polite, but also choose who to let in wisely

Some people, when trying to comfort the griever, end up turning the conversation to how they felt when they're grieving. Others are so obsessed over their image of being helpful when they're not really providing any help, whatsoever. Few actually have the intention of making the griever feel better, but their choice of words couldn't be more wrong. The former category must be dropped. A griever has no time or energy to expend on those who are nosy at best and mean at worst. They already have enough on their plates and must focus on their pain and living through it instead of communicating with insincere individuals. It's also not enough for the latter category to mean well. When the griever experiences discomfort at the mention of something, those listeners should be open to feedback; they should know that they're not helping.

False friendships, and friendships that end

Death and loss have a way of showing grievers who deserves to stay and who should leave. You might be surprised at the number of people who will walk out of your life the minute you become a griever. You already know what we're talking about. Those people who weren't there for you when you most needed the support, they don't deserve to stay, which is why they left. You'd also be surprised at strangers who were much kinder than the permanent fixtures in your life: the family members, the cousins, colleagues, or others. Some people fade out and disappear, while others, you choose to fade out on, because you didn't find in them the support you needed. There will be a lot of people coming in and leaving your life after losing a loved one, and it's completely normal. There will be people who will make you feel small, sad, shamed, or unsupported. These need to go. There will be people who cannot move with you into the next phase of your life, the one where you are grieving, and that's alright. Grief changes people and the relationships and connections that bind them.

Grief and Relationships

Do not try to make other people understand your grief. Don't try to explain what you're feeling to others, what your grief is like. Whether it's valid or not. Your grief is your own, your life is your own, your pain is your own, and no one has the right to judge you or ask you to explain yourself for feeling that way. In order to stop hearing judgments from people, you need to stand your ground. Tell them you are not open to discussing what you're feeling, and you wish to engage in another conversation. If they don't understand that, feel free to end the conversation. You don't need to waste energy on people who won't understand the need for your boundaries or respect them.

Key Takeaway:

Grief will rearrange your relationship with people, and only those who appreciate you and want you to stay true to your own heart, will go through with you.

Reflection Questions:

1. How did your relationship with close people change after your loss?

_____

_____

_____

_____

_____

_____

_____

2. Who did you drop from your life after your loss? Why did you drop
them?

_____

_____

_____

_____

_____

_____

_____

3. Who disappeared from your life after your loss? Why do you think you
never heard back from them?

_____

_____

_____

_____

_____

_____

_____

4. Did you forgive those people who disappeared from your life? Why or why not?

_____

_____

_____

_____

_____

_____

_____

5. Did you ever have to explain your grief to anyone? Why or why not?

_____

_____

_____

_____

_____

_____

_____

Action Step:

Think of your grief as your own property. You can share it with people only you choose, and no one can make you share it without your acceptance. Forgive those who left, and drop those who don't deserve to stay. Right now, only focus on yourself; no one else matters.

Tell yourself the following:

I will keep people who accept my pain and grief in my life.

I will clarify my boundaries with people who don't respect it.

I will redirect the conversation if it is uncomfortable for me.

I will communicate that I'm happy to talk about another subject if people don't respect my wishes.

I will discard people who hold no respect for my privacy.

I will discard people who hold no respect for my pain.

Self-Evaluation:

Evaluate to what extent you can carry out the tips mentioned in the action step, and think thoroughly about your answers to self-reflection questions. Can anything change those answers?

_____

_____

_____

_____

Chapter 14:
Rallying Your Support Team:
Helping Them Help You

This chapter serves as a guide for the support team of the griever. So, if you are grieving, lend this piece to your support team. Communicating your feelings, wants, and needs is too draining, and sometimes, words will fail you.

The first thing supporters want to do is help the griever feel better. They so badly want the griever to snap out of it, to stop feeling bad, and worse yet, they don't really know what to do. There's a huge gap between what they want for the griever and what they actually provide as support. The first thing the supporter needs to realize is that grief is not a problem to be fixed, so they should not come forward with solutions. The griever knows that their pain cannot be fixed. The support team so badly wants the griever to feel better, but there's a miscommunication there. Grief should be viewed as an experience that the griever will have to go through, and then learn to live through, for the rest of their lives. It will not be easy to forget their loved ones, or what life was like when their loved ones were around. As such, grievers should feel companioned and loved inside their own pain and their own grief. That is why the support team should show up and be there for the griever. They should communicate that they don't really know what to do. They won't be able to make things better, but they don't want the griever to be alone either. The following is a list of things that sums up what the support team should and shouldn't do; it will serve as the roadmap to support a griever.

- Don't compare your loss to the griever's, and don't mention who had it worse. This is not a competition, and your loss, even if similar, will simply never be identical to the griever's, simply because grief is unique to each person.

- Ask questions about the griever's experience, what it's like for them, but don't fact check or correct what they're saying, even if it's not accurate. Remember, you're talking to someone whose entire thought pattern shifted, and they can barely sleep, eat, walk, or fulfill their basic needs.

- Let the griever own their experience, and don't hand out your opinion. It's unneeded. Only your support is.

- Don't compliment the griever; they're not facing a self-esteem issue here. Remind the griever that you're there for them, and that they can always lean on you for support.

- Don't be a cheerleader. Walk with them through the laughter and the tears, and mirror their reality back at them. When they mention how awful the situation is, agree with them.

- Don't entice them with thoughts about the future. They're not there, they're in the present moment, and it hurts to be here, and if they shift back to the past, allow them to relive that and live it with them.

- Don't give out suggestions of what might have helped, at least not unless they asked you to, and make sure they're taking care of themselves without you seeming too pushy.

- Understand that even if you're doing everything right, the griever might still ghost you,. Be there for them anyway. Don't take their absence personally; they have a lot on their hands as is.
- Remind the griever that you love them, that you'll never leave their side, and that they can always count on you to be there.

Key Takeaway:

Support can sometimes come in different ways, where people with good intentions might end up making the griever feel worse, while others who give the griever space will be perceived as a true supporter.

Reflection Questions:

1. When your pain was at the higher end of the spectrum, was there someone who supported you through that pain? Who was it?

_____

_____

_____

_____

_____

_____

_____

2. How did that person support you?

_____

_____

_____

_____

_____

_____

_____

3. What was special about that support, and how can you compare it with that of others who tried to be there for you?

_____

_____

_____

_____

_____

_____

_____

4. Was there someone who made you feel guilty for not appreciating the support they gave out? Who was it? Why did they make you feel that, in your opinion?

_____

_____

_____

_____

_____

_____

_____

5. What advice would you add to the list already mentioned in this chapter that make supporters even better ones?

_____

_____

_____

_____

_____

_____

_____

Action Step:

Give out this bullet point list to the close members who are serving as your support system. Ask them to make their own notes about it and be open to any suggestions they make. Also, if there was a person or persons that is were there for you, show them how much you appreciate them by doing something kind for them.

Self-Evaluation:

Once you carry out the action step, monitor your own reaction to your support system's help. Did the list work? Also, how did you feel doing something kind for the person or persons who have been there for you? How did they react?

_____

_____

_____

_____

_____

_____

_____

_____

_____

_____

Part IV
The Way Forward

Chapter 15:
The Tribe of After:
Companionship, True Hope,
and the Way Forward

In grief, you will be alone, but you shouldn't necessarily be lonely. As humans, we are interconnected through the limbic system, through that which cannot be touched, only felt. Devine says that grief is not a test, but an experience of yourself. But it is a test in a way, to see who might stick around, who will be there with you, support you, hold you when the tears come, and listen to you when there are no more tears to be shed. She explains that it's so very difficult for those who did not go through loss to understand what you're passing through. However, there is no household without loss. Everyone has lost someone they love, and that's what connects people to each other: the knowledge that they know a similar, but never identical, kind of pain.

Alone yet not

This is the best time to say that in love, we find companions. In grief, we can find our own tribe. When Devine first lost her Matt, there was no book, no article, no support group online that expressed or communicated the pain that she was passing through, or helped her live through it, deal with it. There were people who were there for her, and others who weren't (which she immediately cut from her life). Even those who so badly wanted to support were not able to, simply because they haven't felt that magnitude of pain that she was experiencing. It only takes a griever to know a griever. Slowly, she found people who understood the kind of grief she was dealing with. That's when she created a community of beautiful grievers who spoke the same language: the language of pain and memories of their loved ones. It helps to know that you are surrounded by people who get the feelings running amok in you. They know better than to judge you for it because they are feeling the very same way.

Connections and communications

Grievers gravitate toward other grievers. They find each other. The loneliness grievers feel among other people who never experienced what they did can draw them to find others who have felt that kind of pain. Devine almost gave up on the field of grief therapy, because she was so tired of being in the pain business. Then, her partner died, so she closed her practice altogether. But she couldn't not go back to it years later. She saw how powerful connection can be after she created her own tribe. She realized that her words made sense to other grievers. While they may not always make grievers feel better, it was enough for her to show fellow grievers that someone out there understands, and they're not alone. As such, she chose to share with them what helped her survive: companionship inside pain, the power of presence, and the magic of love. She communicates that it's incredibly important to find a place where your loss is valued, heard, and honored, especially at a time when your entire center has been ripped from your life. It will be exhausting, putting yourself out there, exposing yourself to the pain, voicing it, seeing it mirrored on others' faces. However, it feels so good to know that you're not alone in your grief. While it will be impossible for anyone to go inside that place where you and your grief alone reside, it's helpful to know that there are people, just like you, struggling with their own grief as well.

Key Takeaway:

Being in grief is a lonely business, but it's not one the griever chooses for themselves. Grievers can find other grievers to share the pain; they deserve to be surrounded by people who speak the same language of pain, after all.

Reflection Questions:

1. What were ways you adapted to help you in your grief?

_____

_____

_____

_____

_____

_____

_____

2. Did you come across people who are grieving? Did you feel any connection to them?

_____

_____

_____

_____

_____

_____

_____

3. If your answer to the previous question was yes, how did connecting with them help you deal with your own grief?

_____

_____

_____

_____

_____

_____

_____

4. How long did it take you to open up to fellow grievers about your grief?

_____

_____

_____

_____

_____

_____

_____

5. Did opening up to other grievers make you more embracing of your own grief? Why or why not?

_____

_____

_____

_____

_____

_____

_____

Action Step:

If you have not yet found your own grief tribe, try to find it. If you couldn't, explore ways in which you can create your own grief tribe. No one deserves to grieve alone. Reach out to grievers online, in person, or in any way you find comfortable and convenient. Virtual support can be just as effective and someone who is in the room with you.

Self-Evaluation:

Evaluate how communicating with fellow grievers made you feel about your grief, and note that down in your journal. Also, write down any thoughts you may have on this chapter's main theme and key takeaway.

_____

_____

_____

_____

_____

_____

_____

_____

_____

_____

_____

_____

Chapter 16:
Love Is the Only Thing That Lasts

There is no denying the fact that the grief you feel when you lose someone is because you loved them. Love and grief are two sides of the same coin. They are those twins who shared the same body, were attached at the hip, could not be separated from each other. When one leaves, the other suffers. There is no preventing grief, because then love would have to cease to exist. What worth would life have if it was lived with no love in it? There is no happy ending to this book, nor there is one to grief. Grief will always, eternally, be painful, and understanding that is the first step to be able to live through it. Even if you don't want to acknowledge love, if you decide to banish it from your life, it is surrounding you as you go, everywhere, and with everyone. It will remain with you for the rest of time, and while its form will change, it will never cease to exist in your life.

It's ok that you're not ok

Love will never fix things. It's not a magical potion that will wipe away all your pains and ease your suffering. But love, alongside companionship, communication, and acknowledgement, will support you in your pain. Having said that, you should know that love will never replace what you've lost, and it won't make being broken any easier.

Exist in the middle ground

Even though Devine dedicated an entire chapter to tell you that, she's repeating it here, in the final chapter, to emphasize its importance. Society tells us that there are only two options in grief. The first is to be eternally sad, huddled in a dark corner, never leaving the house. The second is to put all the sadness behind you and go live a fabulous life. But society never told you that there's a whole life in the middle of those two. That you can create a middle, neutral ground, where you can accept your pain, your grief, your loss, and yet still be your own guide and companion without breaking down every time a memory comes to mind. You can live through the pain by not comparing yourself to who you were before (you're an entirely different person now). You can do that by creating a friendship with your grieving heart, as a result of your experiment with pain. Your heart was broken in ways that can't be fixed. Learn to love yourself anyway. Allow yourself to love that disfigured, broken heart, and speak to others about your heart's state. Doing so will allow other's views on grief and pain to shift, where instead of having people work to 'fix grief', they learn to embrace it, live through it, experiment with it, and help others continue living with it in their lives.

Key Takeaway:

Love and grief are two sides of the same coin. There's no living without love, and grief is the price to be paid for loving.

Reflection Questions:

1. In your opinion, are love and grief similar in a way? Why or why not?

_____

_____

_____

_____

_____

_____

_____

2. What are some ways love can help you move forward with your grief?

_____

_____

_____

_____

_____

_____

_____

3. Do you think life is worth living if love does not exist in it? Why or why not?

_____

_____

_____

_____

_____

_____

4. Have you learned to embrace love in your life, having lost whom you lost?

_____

_____

_____

_____

_____

_____

5. In your opinion, is living a life devoid of love the way people can protect themselves from feeling grief? If so, would life be worth living?

_____

_____

_____

_____

_____

_____

_____

Action Step:

Start thinking of ways love exists in your life. Make a note of that. When you feel ready, share with others the pain of having lost a loved one, and allow them to explore the dimensions grief has by reiterating some of your painful memories. (It is advised to do that only after time has passed when you lost your person, and only when you feel like you can talk about that grief without breaking down.)

Self-Evaluation:

Evaluate how you feel after opening up about your grief. You may choose to write that down in your journal to commemorate it. If you have not been able to open up, what do you think is holding you back? What might be influencing you to stay quiet and not opening up?

All Key Takeaways from It's Ok That You're Not Ok

You have made it to the end of the workbook, and while we are very sad that you have need of this workbook, we are very glad that you chose to embark on this journey of self-discovery and understanding of everything you've been through. Here are all key takeaways from this book:

Chapter One:
The Reality of Loss

The grief, the pain, and all those tumultuous feelings you experienced and are experiencing, they're normal. They will become integrated with your very soul, becoming part of the fabric of your existence.

Chapter Two:
The Second Half of the Sentence:
Why Words of Comfort Feel So Bad

The worst thing a griever can do is allow society to dictate how they should feel about loss, or give a chance for other people to demean their pain.

Chapter Three:
It's Not You, It's Us: Our Models of Grief Are Broken

Your pain is entirely your own, and it has no expiration date, so don't let others dictate why and for how long you feel that pain.

Chapter Four:
Emotional Illiteracy and the Culture of Blame

The world will blame everyone for the loss that happened, but itself. Pain will never be understood and dealt with using the right attitude when people choose to shy away from pain than accept that it's a natural part of life.

Chapter Five:
The New Model of Grief

Grief, just like love, speaks many languages and can serve to unify people everywhere around the world.

Chapter Six:
Living in the Reality of Loss

There is no right way to grief, no right time to donate or remove the lost one's belongings, and no right anything. What is right for a griever will not be for others, and that's alright.

Chapter Seven:
You Can't Solve Grief, but You Don't Have to Suffer

Approaching grief with a mindset of fixing will never work, simply because grief is not a problem to be fixed, but an experience to be lived.

Chapter Eight:
How (and Why) to Stay Alive

Be kind to yourself to take care of it even when you don't want to, because not fixing suffering will only add more pain to what you're already experiencing.

Chapter Nine:
What Happened to My Mind?
Dealing with Grief's Physical Side Effects

Grief will affect the body, brain, and your entire life. Accept that everything in you will change as a result of grief, and that's completely normal.

Chapter Ten:
Grief and Anxiety:
Calming Your Mind When Logic Doesn't Work

Grief has a way of making anxiety run on full blast, making us believe things that aren't there or create scenarios in our minds.

Chapter Eleven:
What Does Art Have to Do with Anything

Creativity is the healthiest way to communicate grief. It can constitute creating different forms of art, writing, photography, cooking, or sculpting.

Chapter Twelve:
Find Your Own Image of Recovery

Grief will change a person, so they become different people after experiencing loss, and even though the world will judge the griever for becoming another person, the griever should focus on constructing a new life for themselves where grief will be a companion.

Chapter Thirteen:
Should You Educate or Ignore Them?

Grief will rearrange your relationship with people, and only those who appreciate you and want you to stay true to your own heart, will go through with you.

Chapter Fourteen:
Rallying Your Support Team: Helping Them Help You

Support can sometimes come in different ways, where people with good intentions might end up making the griever feel worse, while others who give the griever space will be perceived as a true supporter.

Chapter Fifteen:
The Tribe of After:
Companionship, True Hope, and the Way Forward

Being in grief is a lonely business, but it's not one the griever chooses for themselves. Grievers can find other grievers to share the pain; they deserve to be surrounded by people who speak the same language of pain, after all.

Chapter Sixteen:
Love Is the Only Thing That Lasts

Love and grief are two sides of the same coin. There's no living without love, and grief is the price to be paid for loving.

Background Information About Megan Devine

Megan Devine is a psychotherapist, grief advocate, writer and speaker who travels the world encouraging people to open up about their pain and helps grievers understand the reality of their grief by providing insights about it through her experience with it personally and professionally. Her goal is to teach society and the world about how to comfort grievers without jumping in to fix their broken hearts. She lives with an ever-changing band of beasts on a tiny plot of land near the highway in Oregon.

THANK YOU FOR FINISHING THE BOOK!

Looks like you've enjoyed it! :)

We here at Cosmic Publications will always strive to deliver to you the highest quality guides. So, we would like to thank you for supporting us and reading until the very end.

Before you go, would you mind leaving us a review on Amazon? It will mean a lot to us and support us creating high quality guides for you in the future.

JUST SCAN THE CODE BELOW

Thank you again.

Warmly,

The Cosmic Publications Team

Other Workbooks You May Enjoy

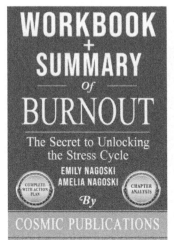

Made in United States
North Haven, CT
29 April 2024

51907206R00089